There are Second Chances

by Miguel Ortiz

PITTSBURGH, PENNSYLVANIA 15238

The contents of this work including, but not limited to, the accuracy of events, people, and places depicted; opinions expressed; permission to use previously published materials included; and any advice given or actions advocated are solely the responsibility of the author, who assumes all liability for said work and indemnifies the publisher against any claims stemming from publication of the work.

All Rights Reserved
Copyright © 2016 by Miguel Ortiz

No part of this book may be reproduced or transmitted, downloaded, distributed, reverse engineered, or stored in or introduced into any information storage and retrieval system, in any form or by any means, including photocopying and recording, whether electronic or mechanical, now known or hereinafter invented without permission in writing from the publisher.

RoseDog Books
585 Alpha Drive, Suite 103
Pittsburgh, PA 15238
Visit our website at *www.rosedogbookstore.com*

ISBN: 978-1-4809-6901-8
eISBN: 978-1-4809-6924-7

Foreword

Two strokes, two flat lines...eight seizures post-stroke.

My first stroke happened at Hilton Head on September 27, 2012. Called an arterial stroke, it was caused by a clog in the artery leading to my brain. The doctors at Hilton Head Regional Hospital said the clog had to be dissolved immediately to avoid certain death. My former wife had to sign a release so they could use a strong medication called tissue plasminogen activator (tpA), which acts quickly but can cause bleeding. Shortly after the medication was administered, I flatlined but was revived by the hospital staff and God's will.

The second stroke occurred on September 29 on the right side of my brain: a cerebral aneurysm. As a result of the bleeding, I was taken by helicopter to the Medical University of South Carolina (MUSC) because Hilton Head Regional did not have the resources to care for me or to do the necessary operation. The bleeding was causing my brain to swell so they had to rush me to MUSC for an immediate craniotomy. Removing a piece of my skull would relieve the swelling.

While at MUSC, I was placed in the intensive care unit (ICU) so the nurses could monitor my vitals all day and night. When they removed the fragment of my skull, it was placed on the right side of my stomach region. It may sound strange but the skull is made of tissue so it needed to be kept in a moist place to preserve it. I flatlined, for the second time, at MUSC for two full minutes. I lost all vital signs, was pronounced clinically dead, and was even given my last rites. I still survived and with God's help, I am here.

I had eight seizures after two strokes and my left side was completely disabled. I'm still unable to use my left hand and leg today. I am now prone to seizures and have to take medicine twice a day to keep them at bay.

I went through a very difficult time but I am still alive and I have adapted to my situation. This is my story and what a journey it has been!

I do many things using only my right hand, including writing this book. The whole process of writing became easier when my publisher, Dorrance, assigned a writer to assist me. I did most of the heavy lifting, writing the majority of the book you're reading, but I thank my assistant immensely for her patience and understanding. Using my right hand only was not easy but I have persevered and most importantly, no matter the difficulty, I am alive.

This is my story, provided to me by my former wife, Marlen, and my friend, John Gajdek. After my first stroke, I passed out and don't remember much until I woke up two weeks later at the Shepard Center Hospital in Atlanta, so I rely heavily on their accounts of what occurred.

You cannot reverse the clock when things go wrong; you can only move forward and keep the faith. Life is about ups and downs and it's how you deal with the downs that defines you. "When the going gets tough, the tough get going" is my motto, something drilled into me during my time in the Marine Corps. Now that I have come to deep faith in God, I also believe the saying, "God helps those who help themselves". But I add something to it: I believe God helps those who follow His commandments in an attempt to be good people. In my case, becoming a born-again Christian after my stroke has had a huge impact on my life and helped me during this difficult time. I am convinced that Christ my Lord and Savior gave me a second chance to live in the flesh. We are all spirits living in human bodies:

> *And if the Spirit of him who raised Jesus from the dead is living in you, he who raised Christ from the dead will also give life to your mortal bodies because of his Spirit who lives in you. Therefore, brothers and sisters, we have an obligation—but it is not to the flesh, to live according to it. For if you live according to the flesh, you will die; but if by the Spirit you put to death the misdeeds of the body, you will live.* **Romans 8: 11-13, NIV**

Introduction

How do you explain tragedy, miracle, and recovery in a three-year span? I have only one explanation and that is God. **John 10: 27:** *"My sheep listen to my voice; I know them, and they follow me."* I have been disobedient by not following the rules of God. God is no different from our parents; if we disobey, we get punished. **Hebrews 3: 9-10:** *"...where your ancestors tested and tried me, though for forty years they saw what I did. That is why I was angry with that generation; I said, 'Their hearts are always going astray, and they have not known my ways.'"* The Bible is our "Basic Instructions Before Leaving Earth."

I am paying for my sins. I believe God is no different from our parents in some respects. If we disobey we get punished. It's as simple as that. God is our spiritual father and, as such, we are all related—brothers and sisters in Christ—which makes us a pretty big family. Christmas and Thanksgiving just got expensive and became standing room only, especially with the world's population, as of March 12, 2015, standing at 7 billion. In the Bible, God instructs us on how to live successfully so we can all be at peace. I am an example of His good deeds and of how He cares and loves us all.

There are certainly a lot of different viewpoints on this truth. Faith can be very elusive—our world is all about 'seeing is believing'—so when you don't believe, following His instructions as outlined in the Bible can be challenging. The Ten Commandments are a start. There are more than ten commandments, though. In fact the number is actually closer to 600. But the main commandment is to LOVE. The Bible, with Moses' Old Testament and Jesus Christ's New Testament, provide guidance for their closest disciples. The apostle Paul wrote 13 books in the New Testament and he was very close to Jesus Christ.

Disobedience (sinning) is a serious matter for God, perpetuated by Satan, that we continue to neglect. See the book of Genesis! Satan tempted Eve to eat the fruit from the tree of knowledge; fruit that God instructed Adam not to touch or eat. And when they ate the fruit anyway, they were punished severely.

In this book I will reference scripture from the Life Application Study Bible, New International Version. There are different versions in distribution, however none of them compromise the word of God so you don't have to read the same one I do. What is important is to study the Bible. We will be that much better off for it—I know I am! I study and meditate with His word day and night to learn how I can be a better person, and now I am at peace with no self-pity or feeling sorry for myself.

God's words of instruction are outlined in the book of Joshua with all the distractions and violence we face each day. **Joshua 1: 7-9:**

> *Be strong and very courageous. Be careful to obey all the law my servant Moses gave you; do not turn from it to the right or to the left, that you may be successful wherever you go. Keep this Book of Instructions always on your lips; meditate on it day and night, so that you may be careful to do everything written in it. Then you will be prosperous and successful. Have I not commanded you? Be strong and courageous. Do not be afraid; do not be discouraged, for the Lord your God will be with you wherever you go.*

Satan thrives on this and it is his goal. Just as God has a plan for us that ismostly good,so also does Satan have a plan for us that ismostly bad. He enacted his plan in the garden of Eden and we can see what the results were in Genesis:

> *And I will put enmity between you and the woman, and between your offspring[a] and hers; he will crush[b] your head, and you will strike his heel." To the woman he said, "I will make your pains in childbearing very severe; with painful labor you will give birth to children. Your desire will be for your husband, and he will rule over you." To Adam he said,*

> *"Because you listened to your wife and ate fruit from the tree about which I commanded you, 'You must not eat from it,'* "*Cursed is the ground because of you; through painful toil you will eat food from it all the days of your life. It will produce thorns and thistles for you, and you will eat the plants of the field. By the sweat of your brow you will eat your food until you return to the ground, since from it you were taken; for dust you are and to dust you will return.* **Genesis 3: 15-19, NIV**

Satan might not appear to you in the form of a serpent with a physical temptation, but he still has a plan for mankind's destruction. The following areas are Satan's goals against God's children:

1) Doubt—makes you question God's word and His goodness

2) Discouragement—makes you look at your problems rather than God

3) Diversion/Temptation—makes the wrong things seem attractive to you so you will want them more than the right things

4) Defeat—makes you feel like a failure so you don't even try

5) Delay—makes you put off something so that it never gets done

6) Shame—makes you feel guilty that you worry about how others feel about you instead of apologizing and asking for forgiveness, others will appreciate you more if you ask for forgiveness and this is how God makes you shameless.

God provides for all of His children and He uses different methods to accomplish His good deeds. In my case, it was more of a wake-up call for me to get my act together. I am certain God was sending me a message and the message was, "You need to change your ways and I will bring you into my kingdom." God provided me with a second chance to be a better person by following all of His rules.

So we have to ask ourselves: are we avoiding Satan or assisting him? God made sure I would become a better person so I could continue living in the flesh here on earth. The spirit that is within you is controlled by God. It is the spirit that we need to pray to and ask for his forgiveness. We are all spirits living in the flesh and He will help:

> *Those who live according to the flesh have their minds set on what the flesh desires; but those who live in accordance with the Spirit have their minds set on what the Spirit desires. The mind governed*

> *by the flesh is death, but the mind governed by the Spirit is life and peace. The mind governed by the flesh is hostile to God; it does not submit to God's law, nor can it do so. Those who are in the realm of the flesh cannot please God. You, however, are not in the realm of the flesh but are in the realm of the Spirit, if indeed the Spirit of God lives in you. And if anyone does not have the Spirit of Christ, they do not belong to Christ. But if Christ is in you, then even though your body is subject to death because of sin, the Spirit gives life because of righteousness. And if the Spirit of him who raised Jesus from the dead is living in you, he who raised Christ from the dead will also give life to your mortal bodies because of his Spirit who lives in you.* **Romans 8: 5-11, NIV.**

You cannot ask for help and forgiveness and continue to do the same things by following Satan, who tries to control the flesh, especially if he knows you have no faith in God (sin is in the flesh Satan works on daily to control us, although I know this is not important to non- believers or atheists).

But I am alive and this is my story and my opinion. I know God didn't want me in His kingdom until He felt I was ready for eternal life (heaven), at least by His standards. That is why He has given me a second chance to correct my sins. God never abandoned me or us; I or we abandoned Him. God gives everyone a second chance, just like our parents give us second chances to correct our faults. God will do the same for anyone that embraces Him and His laws.

My eldest son said to me one day when I was trying to read a verse of the Bible to him, "Dad, I don't believe in the Bible. I don't have to read it to be a good person."

I said to him, "You are not alone in not believing this. It is a problem with humans globally. There are many people on earth who feel the same way, but being a good person is the entire premise of the Bible. Good people do good things and love one another; there is no bitterness, quarreling, killing, stealing or lying; just love, caring, and giving. If you study the Bible carefully you will be surprised at the love God shares with us."

Just to be clear, God does not want to hurt us. After all, we are His children. **Ephesians 6: 1-7:**

> *Children, obey your parents in the Lord, for this is right. "Honor your father and mother"—which is the first commandment with a promise—"so that it may go well with you and that you may enjoy long life on the earth." Fathers, do not exasperate your children; instead, bring them up in the training and instruction of the Lord.*

Chapter One – Tragedy

It was a clear and pleasant day on Thursday, September 27, 2012; a normal day for me. I got up, showered, and prepared for my trip to Hilton Head for a friend's wedding and for a weekend of golf.

In late August, I had accepted my friend Tim Corlis' wedding invitation. The event was to be held September 29 at Hilton Head. Tim called me to ensure I was coming because he wanted to play golf the day before the wedding, that Friday the 28th, and he knew I enjoyed golf. A week prior, I discussed the trip with my friend, John Gadjek. I don't know why or what compelled me to invite him on our trip. In fact, it's still a question I ask myself, especially since John and his wife, Deanna, did not know the wedding couple and were not invited to the wedding. John and Deanna were not comfortable at first.

I now feel that God wanted John there—it was a form of divine intervention. It so happens that my friend Tim had last minute cancelations—divine intervention at work again. I asked Tim if John and Deanna could also attend with us. At the time, I thought it would be a good idea but my wife did not agree that, as friends, we could enjoy the golfing. I have no explanation for why I asked John if he and Deanna wanted to go down with my wife Marlen and I to make it a golf weekend and mini vacation break.

John was okay with it, but needed to speak to Deanna first to get her thoughts on a few logistics like who would take care of their daughter, Taylor, who would need a sitter for the weekend, and the customers from his landscaping business. Friday through Sunday were peak days for the business. John was okay with the idea of going to Hilton Head. Besides, he liked the golf courses there. John and Deanna decided to go with us and he even volunteered to drive if I would pay for gas—which I don't remember paying for—because he had a truck that could accommodate all the luggage and clubs going with us.

John did not know Tim but when Tim happened to call me to confirm that Marlen and I were coming, I took the liberty of asking Tim if it would be okay for John and his wife to join us. Tim was gracious enough to say that John and his wife were welcome.

Chapter Two – Miracle

It all started with John, sitting by my side. He was driving the golf cart while I was sitting on the passenger side during my first stroke, which happened that Thursday, September 27, in the afternoon at the Kupp Golf Course at Hilton Head.

John recognized the signs of an oncoming stroke: the left side of my face was drooping and my speech was slurred. He asked me to either swallow or spit out the remaining part of the turkey sandwich I was still chewing on John says I laid down on my side and opened my mouth wide enough for him to clear it out. As a former paramedic and police officer in North Carolina, he knew how to handle the situation. While on duty, he would be asked to care for stroke victims.

Divine intervention came in the form of a maintenance person who saw we were having problems. He drove by in his maintenance cart and asked John if we were okay and John said to him, "Don't go anywhere, I may need you." John immediately called 911.

While in the golf cart, John said I was resting my head on the arm rest of the cart and looking up at the clear blue sky, from which I saw a bright light as I lay there. From the bright light, I heard a voice say to me, "Miguel, it's not your turn." I did not see a person or body, or know if I was totally hallucinating. I just heard the voice - divine intervention again. The brain is the operating system for the body, an amazing organ—again, a second chance.

> **John 10: 27-30:** *My sheep listen to my voice; I know them, and they follow me. I give them eternal life, and they shall never perish; no one will snatch them out of my hand. My Father, who has given them to me, is greater than all; no one can snatch them out of my Father's hand. I and the Father are one.*

There is a God. This is my belief as I have experienced what I believe to be a supernatural occurrence.

John and I had played one hole that was a par four. The second hole was a par five and we had teed off and hit our second shots. On the second, I cleared the hazard but John did not. That's when we returned to the golf cart. I remember John's encounter with the maintenance man and my own experience with the bodiless voice. That is as much as I can remember. I never saw a person, a silhouette, or anything that could be described as human.

When I finally woke up at Shepherd Center Hospital in Atlanta, I asked John about my recollection, wanting to know if it was correct. He said everything was correct but the part where he hit his second shot into the hazard on the second hole which I did not warn him about. We had teed off and I knew about the hazard ahead of us. If a person did not hit long or faded righ,t the person could reach the hazard. John was a long hitter so I did not reference the hazard and, since I had played the course before and we had a bet on the match between us, I had a memory lapse, maybe due to my oncoming stroke.

I had passed out from my first stroke, and the next time I woke up, I was lying on a bed at Shepherd Center Hospital in Atlanta.

Chapter Three – Recovery

At the hospital, I was diagnosed with having had an arterial stroke. The main artery leading to my brain was clogged and they informed my wife that they would have to administer the tpA. My wife was more interested in my health and ensuring that I would survive this more than the liability, so she signed. Then I started to hemorrhage and my brain started swelling. I also had my first flatline.

As I am finishing this book, I am still recovering. Recovery for me meant regaining some of my independence so I could do things like bathe, go to the bathroom, and be able to walk on my own. I do walk, but with a cane, and I am fortunate because I can see, speak, think, and express myself, whereas most stroke victims don't have these functions that we take for granted.

God made sure I was surrounded by family, friends, and professionals to help me recover. Once I got more confident and healthier, my sons asked if I could move back to Atlanta from Orlando so they could see me more often and help me get better. My oldest son is a personal trainer at Lifetime Fitness. He manages their Southeast Region and I don't mean to sound biased, but he is an excellent trainer. His clients swear by him so be on the lookout for him. He will have a website coming out soon that will give you both physical and nutritional information. It's not expensive when you compare his rates to how much it costs to stay healthy these days.

My sister, Elizabeth, was able to find a home assistance living residence with the help of my good friend, Lillian Klook. I lived on my own for a year at the residence, called Dunwoody Pines, where I was fortunate to meet Alison Gitten, a good Christian caretaker. She helped me get to my doctor's appointments, helped me with my laundry, and one day she had to call 911 as I was having a seizure—my seventh.

After that year at Dunwoody, I moved in with my son Alejandro in Apharetta, GA. While I was at Dunwoody, I proved to myself and others that I could be more independent, but Alejandro wanted to care for me. He wanted to see me through the doctor visits and rehab and, once again, this seemed like divine intervention.

Chapter Four – Professionals

Doctors, surgeons, therapists

I worked with three types of therapists. First, there are physical therapists to help me walk. Second, occupational therapists help me use and strengthen my weak arm; for me, it was my left arm and hand. They also help me to use the strong arm with proven techniques to dress, bathe, and groom myself. The stroke occurred on the right side of my brain, which made recovery on my left arm and leg challenging, particularly my arm. Because of subluxation on my left side, my left shoulder and arm are detached, making it difficult to recover the movement I had in my arm prior to my strokes. With exercise, I can improve my arm movement by working the muscles in my left arm and shoulder. Once the muscles are attached again, it will be easier to send signals from my brain to my left side, which is how the brain works. It sends brain signals through our nervous system. The brain has the ability to generate what neurologists call 'new wires' that find a way from the brain to the affected area—it's called rerouting—to provide the functionality I had prior to the strokes(i.e. driving, eating and walking). Third, speech therapists help me with speech and other deficiencies.

I had what they called left dyslexic vision. The vision in my left eye was impacted so I had difficulty seeing out of it or paying attention to my left side. The brain works like a computer.It gets used to how you use your body functions and the body instantly performs those actions when called upon by the brain. The speech therapists were helpful in getting me to concentrate on my left side and now I am able to see more clearly.

It's not like it used to be but I have come a long way from being bed-ridden and wheelchair-bound to walking with a cane, getting dressed, going to the bathroom and bathing; all the things we take for granted. I know I will prevail and God will help. He has not given up on me, nor will I give up on him or on all the people who have helped me. There is something to be said about resiliency and determination and if anything, I am stronger spiritually and this is a good thing. While it is still a challenge for me to do what I was used to before (driving a car, playing golf, using my left side, walking, and running), I am just happy to be alive in the flesh and to see my sons regularly and, hopefully, grandchildren one day down the road.

God is not through with me yet. When I started to embrace God, I changed a lot. It motivated me to try to get back to normal and do what the doctors said I could not do. Prior to the stroke, I did not believe in or have faith in God. This has all changed since I heard the voice say to me, "It's not your turn, Miguel," and survived certain death. My faith in God became stronger when I started going with my sister, Elizabeth, to her church, Christ is Victory, in Orlando, Florida and meeting her pastors, Juan and Naomi Alvarez.

Naomi said when she first met me, "You will walk again, but you must believe and have faith." I started to attend mass regularly on Sundays with Elizabeth. I would go in my wheelchair. I had a special van that I got in Georgia that was wheelchair accessible and the ushers always saved a spot for me where I could fit comfortably. My sister would also use my van to transport me to therapy in Georgia at Pathway, a therapy subsidiary of Shepherd Hospital. Since it was outpatient, my insurance covered the additional therapy. When my insurance expired, I left Georgia to go live with my sister in Orlando. She could care for me when my wife could not..

When I moved to Florida, I went to Celebration Hospital where I resumed therapy. When I left Georgia to live with my sister, my mom and sisters came to visit me, which was a relief for Elizabeth because getting me in and out of the van was a challenge. But she was a trooper and was determined to get me to therapy, doctors, shopping, and church on Sundays.

In late August 2013, Pastor Naomi Alvarez asked me to come to the front of the stage as she was at the pulpit delivering her sermon. Then she asked me to stand in front of my wheelchair, which I could do. At this point, she came down and stood on my right side and asked me to put my right arm around her neck and shoulder and to lean on her. She asked me to walk and I took my first steps as she supported my weight. At the time, I weighed 178 pounds but since she was holding me up completely by herself, the dead weight of my body was 356 pounds I took my first steps after my stroke with her; we walked about fifty feet.

The next day I had therapy with Tina, my physical therapist at Florida Celebration Hospital. I explained to Tina what had happened at church and then she went to retrieve a four-pronged cane. She instructed me on how to use it because there is a sequence you must follow to use it properly. All of this happened in August and September of 2013, one year after my stroke. Tina went further and showed me how to walk up and down stairs carefully, too. Therapists are big on safety and she took all the precautions necessary.

I also realized, through therapy and faith, that I could regain my ability to once again walk normally and even run, drive, and play golf. In addition to meeting my pastors, Naomi and Juan, I received a lot of support from the church members who were always praying for me and cheering me on at church. Through therapy and my newfound faith, I could recover. Now it was up to me and my hard work. I just had to believe and have faith.

The Shepherd Center Pastor, during one of his rounds, asked me if I would like to attend mass. Pre-stroke, I would not have considered it. All this had changed for me and it was a chance to regroup. I did go and my sons, on occasion, would join me.

Chapter Five – Family

My family is the best. They are supportive, loving, kind, and, since day one, they have all gone out of their way to pitch in and help me when needed. They have all made this journey possible and all deserve my gratitude but I can't say enough about my sister, Elizabeth, in particular. She is an angel sent to me by God who took care of me for almost two years by taking me to therapy, doctor's appointments, cooking, helping me with bills and medication, and being my advocate in every way and at every turn. Basically, she did everything for me that I could no longer do for myself. She did so much but she wasn't alone.

My mom, at 81, would fuss over me like I was a newborn. In fact, at one point, I even said to her, "Stop treating me like a baby."

She responded, "You will always be my baby."

A mother's love is so impressive that I still don't have a response but I love her dearly. I also have two extended families, the Lugos and the Kloocks, who pitched in when they could, as well. The Lugos live in Snellville, Georgia and I have known them for over 40 years. They are wonderful people—loving and caring—and I thank them.

I also want to extend special thanks to my cousin, Judy, who cared for me when needed and who also helped my former wife, who had a tough call to make that got me to this point. She needed a shoulder to lean on when she was making the decision to allow the doctors at Hilton Head to administer the medication that wound up determining whether or not I could reach this point in my life. Even though I experienced divine intervention during my stroke and knew that God would bring me through this for a greater purpose prior to her decision, my wife did not know what I had heard during my first stroke and had no such assurance.

To my cousins in New York, Florida, California and Georgia, I love and thank you all. There are so many of you that I can't name everyone but your love and support have helped me more than you can know.

I know my sister-in-law, Maria, has also been an angel to my family. She lost her husband—my brother—on May 17, 2014, but she gave him 12 additional years by caring for him. He was very ill for years before passing but she was there for him in every aspect from nutrition to physical assistance and emotional support. I know Maria, my nephew—also my godson—and Maria's family, who adopted my brother as their own and loved him dearly, miss him terribly, as do I. I will always be grateful for the love that she and her family showed to him. I learned from Maria that a spouse can be a best friend and soulmate, as well as a spouse. I know there is also the danger that faces married couples of simply becoming acquaintances and the difference is the actual things you do from the heart. Close family and friends don't feel sorry for one another. They are saddened by the circumstances but show their love by motivating one another, getting involved, showing kindness and concern and when possible, and lending a helping hand. I am so grateful for all those who showed me true friendship and familial love during this difficult time.

Chapter Six – Friends

A friend is someone you trust and can depend on. Someone who is there for you and reaches out often to help when needed. This is a tough call because I have friends in New York, Georgia, and Florida. I have Ela Alayon, who worked for me in Miami, and Hilda Collazo, who worked for me in New York but is now living in Orlando. I want to thank the Polo Golf and Country Club members in Cumming, Georgia because, while I was not destitute after my stroke, they showed concern and generosity. I truly have many great friends and, while I was disappointed in a few people during my sickness and recovery, I will keep that to myself.

    I can say that John is a hero to my family. He and Deanna hung in there with me in the hospitals, both Hilton Head and MUSC, until I woke up from my strokes. They both continually supported me and my wife. I really appreciated it and want to thank them both for their concern and help when it was needed most.

I have a special friend in New York, Sally Borkland, who worked for me and has continued to reach out to me weekly to check in and ask if there is anything I need. Others also check in on me including Mike Tannian, Arthur Dimella, and Tim Corliss, whose wedding I never made it to because of my stroke. He says I did it on purpose because I didn't want to give him a wedding gift. I say I didn't want to kick his butt in golf in front of his new wife. Tim is a good egg and someone I kibitz with all the time. He is a good friend.

I also lost my aunt, someone who was both a friend and second mother to me, who always gave me advice. She passed away seven years ago but she used to tell me, "Miguel, friends are a dollar in the pocket. I don't have that problem."

My mom would say, "Show me who your friends are and I'll show you who you are." She's very proud of me.

Thank you all, my friends. I can't wait to get back out on the golf course. In fact, I have a few bets to settle when I get there.

I don't worry if family or friends don't or can't call or reach out to me. Life goes on and these are my expectations. Everyone knows this—I have had friends and relatives leave me and go on to God and I moved on with my life, but they are always in my thoughts . That's how they want it to be and so do I.

I thank you, Jay Smith. Thanks for your friendship and help. Speaking of my friends at Polo Golf Club, I would be remiss if I did not mention the "Mo rule." Mo is a nickname given to me by Wayne Palmore. It stands for Miguel Ortiz and he made it up when I played in the MYERS group at Polo and was fortunate enough to win a few dollars. Rich Ketchum used to call me 'Mo Money,' the ATM that made withdrawals instead of deposits. When we had tournaments at the club, everyone would donate five dollars for one raffle ticket or we would purchase five raffle tickets for twenty dollars. When the ticket number was drawn, the money we collected would be split 50/50. Half would go to the men's golf association and the other half to the lucky raffle ticket holder. When playing golf, I think I won this raffle about five times so the board members decided I would pull the raffle tickets to ensure I would not win again. That was Mo rule number one.

After playing 18 holes on Saturdays, we would usually stick around to see if anyone wanted to play an E-9(extra nine holes) along with a game called Wolf. Usually, about four or five guys would play an E-9. The line-up would change each week although there were the usual suspects who were almost always there. One Saturday in particular it was myself, Jay Smith, John Gajdek, Rick Ketchum, Troy, Blane Eldridge and Wayne Palmore. Whoever was the "wolf," when we played this way, would decide if he wanted to contend for the hole by himself or choose another person to compete against the others. The selected person could bow out if he wanted, but that didn't happen often. We played each hole for a small bet of four dollars for the hole and four dollars for the trash, birdies, sandies, and closest to pins on par 3s. By the time we got to hole E-6(the old #16, because the course had been given upgrades so they changed the numbers, ten was changed to one and one to ten)on the back nine, the person who was furthest behind could choose to leave the bet the same or halve the bet depending on how much you were behind.

Our money standings were announced by Rick Ketchum and, on that day, I was behind the most at $32. I never said anything to the rest of the guys about this, but Rick said to me, "Mo, you're down $32, what do you want to do?"

While I didn't care at all about the money, something about the way he said it bothered me. Rick had this smirk on his face that seemed to say the ATM would be making deposits for once and I decided to halve the bet and make it $16 for the hole and $16 for the trash. Wayne Palmore was my partner for the next three holes and we won them all. I hit my drive down the center on the last hole, #18, and Blane was the "wolf" but he didn't choose me. I told him I was going to win the hole with a birdie and Wayne couldn't have been happier because I did exactly that.

When we finished, Rick tallied up the winnings and the losses. I had gone from $32 down to over $100 up. Since then, the bet cannot exceed the minimum and "Mo rule" number two is invoked every time they play Wolf on an E9. I was kind to my friends that day and decided not to collect, but Rick better remember never to mess with Mo Money!

I know this story isn't relevant, but it's a funny anecdote that I wanted to share about my friends. I think golfers will appreciate knowing I birdied 16 and 18, Wayne birdied 16 and 17, and Rick was beside himself tallying up the bets. Jay said to me, "You have some guts, and you took the smirks off our faces!"

I have not played golf since the stroke. It's been over three years now and I miss the game and my friends, but I know I am lucky to be alive. Thank you, Lord, for being with us in many ways. There is no better guardian angel to have!

I know those who know me are rolling their eyes because they know I was no angel. I won't deny that. Yes, I partied and went clubbing. I got drunk, flirted with other women, chased trouble, I was reckless, didn't go to church, got high on drugs, and was unfaithful to my wife. I was consumed by the devil and his direction, desiring what the flesh wanted instead of the spirit, but God saw something in me and decided it wasn't my turn. He decided to save me instead.

I remember, as a teenager, I would leave the house at night and not come home until the early hours of the next day. That was during the week. On weekends it was even worse. I would spend my time with friends who were part of gangs and go to parties to make out with girls and dance (dirty dancing is too tame a term for what we did). It was more like safe sex than dancing. I know that if I had been exposed at that time in my life to the things kids are exposed to today, I would be a great grandfather by now. But when you accept Jesus as your Lord and Savior, none of your former terrible deeds define you anymore. God brings you out of the dark world and back into the light. Salvation is a roller coaster ride I never expected to ride. I would never have guessed God's plan for me.

To a very dear couple and very dear friends, Larry and Lillian Kloock, I can't thank you enough for your love and kindness. It was Lillian who helped my wife get me into Shepherd Center hospital, which is the best inpatient rehabilitation facility in the United States. Her generosity, I'm convinced, was divine intervention. Lillian and her family were always there for me; I felt like they adopted me. As for Larry, I want my putter back! The magic wand only works for the wizard and that would be me. Honestly, Larry has already returned my putter but I haven't been able to use it yet. Larry couldn't use it either, but if he could putt, he would be on the Senior Tour by now.

I want to dedicate this book to many people. First and foremost are my sons, Miguel and Alejandro, who I love unconditionally and who keep me grounded. I miss my cousin, Lorraine Gonzalez, who was an angel here on earth and now is a special angel for God in heaven. She left us too soon: December 10, 2014. She is now with my brother, my aunt, and her grandmother, Carmen Ortiz, who joined God in 2007. I miss you all but your spirits will live on in eternity with God, which is a pretty great deal. And as we all know: everything happens for a reason.

Finally, I also dedicate this book to my two church families and, particularly, the pastors. In Cumming, Georgia, I attend The Vine with Pastor John Adams. In Orlando, I also attend Christ is Victory with pastors, Juan and Naomi Alvarez. It has been a pleasure to hear your sermons and to get to know you all personally. You are God's children and I thank you. The following passages from scripture have helped me get through this time and I wouldn't have them if I didn't have my pastors:

Psalm 46: 1 *"God is our refuge and strength, an ever-present help in trouble."*

Hebrews 6: 9-16:
Even though we speak like this, dear friends, we are convinced of better things in your case—the things that have to do with salvation. God is not unjust; he will not forget your work and the love you have shown him as you have helped his people and continue to help them. We want each of you to show this same diligence to the very end, so that what you hope for may be fully realized. We do not want you to become lazy, but to imitate those who through faith and patience inherit what has been promised. When God made his promise to Abraham, since there was no one greater for him to swear by, he swore by himself, saying, 'I will surely bless you and give you many descendants.' And so after waiting patiently, Abraham received what was promised. People swear by someone greater than themselves, and the oath confirms what is said and puts an end to all argument.

John 15: 1-5:
'I am the true vine, and my Father is the gardener. He cuts off every branch in me that bears no fruit, while every branch that does bear fruit he prunes

so that it will be even more fruitful. You are already clean because of the word I have spoken to you. Remain in me, as I also remain in you. No branch can bear fruit by itself; it must remain in the vine. Neither can you bear fruit unless you remain in me. I am the vine; you are the branches. If you remain in me and I in you, you will bear much fruit; apart from me you can do nothing.'

I love you guys; what a joy you are to me!

One final word: we are always wondering why some friends or family members leave us. It's a question that puts doubts in our minds. But it isn't God working against us. It is part of Satan's master plan. God is with us all the time and just because you don't see him doesn't mean he isn't there. We don't see the air around us either, but we can breathe so we know it's there. Join God! I have and I can assure you that He won't mislead you. In God we trust and if you didn't, then you would donate all your money to good causes, because you carry those words in your pockets, wallets, purses and keep them in your bank accounts every day. But so do atheists and nonbelievers.

The truth hurts and the pain is what woke me up. I pray it will wake you up, too. I pray for all of you daily whether you are in the midst of the good, the bad, or the ugly. Prayers don't have to be long; you just need to get to the point. That's what Jesus Christ did when he prayed, "Father, forgive them, for they know not what they do." When I pray, I keep it simple (1). "God, please take care of my friends, their families, and mine."

If I left anyone out, it was not purposeful. I just don't want to write two hundred chapters. God bless you! I thank you if you took the time to read my story. I would like to help good causes like peace and love on earth for all. We need more hugging and less fighting. We need to be donating to good causes like churches, families, and those who need and can use the support. We have children in need as well as soldiers, the men and women who fight for our freedom. I am not interested in profiting in any way and just want to help where I can, like my churches do. God does not want us to drift through life. He wants us to influence people for Him just like Lot did in Genesis. If God is with us, who can be against us?

A special thanks to Dorrance Publishing and the consultant and ghost writer they provided for me, who helped orchestrate the updating, editing, and publishing of my book as a novice.

---

(1) Joyce Meyer, *The Power of Being Thankful*, page 189.

Chapter Seven

The brain weighs three pounds and is the cause of 140,000 deaths each year. The highest cause is the lack of blood flow and oxygen to the brain, which leads to a stroke. The brain is the operating system for the entire central nervous system. In the Bible, in the book of Genesis, it says "a blow to the head is fatal," but, "a strike to the heel is not as damaging." For example, a broken arm or leg will heal in a matter of months, whereas a traumatic injury to the brain will take away abilities in other parts of the body that will or can make them useless. The impact to the body and its abilities as we are accustomed to them is unfathomable if you haven't seen it yourself.

The brain has one billion neurons that independently have over 100 functions *each*. They control all of our organs, muscles, blood vessels, all of our senses and our skeletal structure. The brain needs oxygen to survive. It uses twenty percent of the blood and oxygen in your body and going for five to ten minutes without oxygen will result in permanent damage. The moral of the story is: take care of your head and lungs. Your health is very important to you and your family. You could be a billionaire but without your health you might as well be penniless. Don't take it for granted. The right side of the brain controls the left side of the body and also creativity, emotion, recognition, intuition, and imagination. Fortunately for me, the latter has had very little impact on me. Divine intervention.

Epilogue

There are friends, family, and associates who feel I have been given a bad break but I don't agree. On the contrary, I feel I have been given a gift — a second chance at a new life. I can now live life in a better way. I am no longer living in the dark consumed by hatred, greed, evil, power, and coveting what others have. These are all satanic attributes but, instead of being controlled by those impulses, I now live in the light. My eyes are open to the good and the love we can all have. Try to love your neighbor as you love yourself including the good, the bad, and the ugly, even in your enemy. This is one of God's most important commandments. Such a simple statement can change the course of this world.

Why are we afraid of peace and love? I'll admit my reasons for wanting those are selfish. I want my children, grandchildren, and great grandchildren to live in peace and harmony and I don't think that's too much to ask. Romans 5: 1-6:

> *Therefore, since we have been justified through faith, we have peace with God through our Lord Jesus Christ, through whom we have gained access by faith into this grace in which we now stand. And we boast in the hope of the glory of God. Not only so, but we also glory in our sufferings, because we know that suffering produces perseverance; perseverance, character; and character, hope. And hope does not put us to shame, because God's love has been poured out into our hearts through the Holy Spirit, who has been given to us. You see, at just the right time, when we were still powerless, Christ died for the ungodly.*

We are all brothers and sisters, yet we have nothing but disdain and contempt for each other. If we treated each other as family, we would be closer to love, peace, and harmony, and more importantly, a world at rest. Think about it: when tragedy occurs the first words or text are 'Oh my God,' OMG, is he really?'. When we do good it's, 'Thank you Lord,' or 'praise the Lord'. Athletes say on camera all the time that their talents are God-given, and that's true. The Creator gave us everything in our lives and our environment and as a world, we continue to destroy and pollute it. God bless you, my brothers and sisters. Let's pass it along—what a novel idea. I am so blessed to be given a second chance.